Food Field Trips

Let's Explore
Tomatoes!

Jill Colella

Lerner Publications ◆ Minneapolis

Hello Friends,

Everybody eats, even from birth. This is why learning about food is important. Making the right choices about what to eat begins with knowing more about food. Food literacy helps us to be more curious about food and adventurous about what we eat. In short, it helps us discover how delicious the world of food can be.

When I was young, my grandma let me pick tiny tomatoes from her garden. Warm from the sun, they were so full of flavor. That is one of my favorite food memories. Do you have a memory of something tasting so fresh?

For more inspiration, ideas, and recipes, visit www.teachkidstocook.com.

Jill

About the Author
Happy cook, reformed picky eater, and long-time classroom teacher, Jill Colella founded both *Ingredient* and *Butternut*, award-winning children's magazines that promote food literacy.

Lerner Publications Company
An imprint of Lerner Publishing Group, Inc.
241 First Avenue North
Minneapolis, MN 55401 USA

For reading levels and more information, look up this title at www.lernerbooks.com.

Main body text set in Mikado
Typeface provided by HVD

Library of Congress Cataloging-in-Publication Data
Names: Colella, Jill, author.
Title: Let's explore tomatoes! / Jill Colella.
Description: Minneapolis : Lerner Publications, 2020. | Series: Food field trips | Includes bibliographical references and index. | Audience: Ages 4–8 | Audience: Grades K–1 | Summary: "Ripe and juicy, tomatoes are a welcome sign of summer! Inspire food literacy in young readers by showing them how tomatoes are grown and harvested. Includes a recipe for an easy tomato sauce"– Provided by publisher.
Identifiers: LCCN 2019052410 (print) | LCCN 2019052411 (ebook) | ISBN 9781541590328 (library binding) | ISBN 9781728402857 (paperback) | ISBN 9781728400228 (ebook)
Subjects: LCSH: Tomatoes—Juvenile literature.
Classification: LCC SB349 .C66 2020 (print) | LCC SB349 (ebook) | DDC 635/.642—dc23

LC record available at https://lccn.loc.gov/2019052410
LC ebook record available at https://lccn.loc.gov/2019052411

Manufactured in the United States of America
1 – CG – 7/15/20

SCAN FOR BONUS CONTENT!

Table of Contents

Picture Glossary

flowers

ripe

sauce

seeds

seedlings

ALL ABOUT TOMATOES

Tomatoes can be eaten raw, like on a sandwich or in salsa.

Tomatoes can also be cooked into sauces. Pizza sauce is made with tomatoes. So is ketchup!

LET'S COMPARE

Tomatoes come in many colors, shapes, and sizes.

Some are sweet and juicy.
Some are tart or tangy.

Tomatoes can be small and round or big and bumpy.

LET'S EXPLORE

Tomatoes grow on plants.

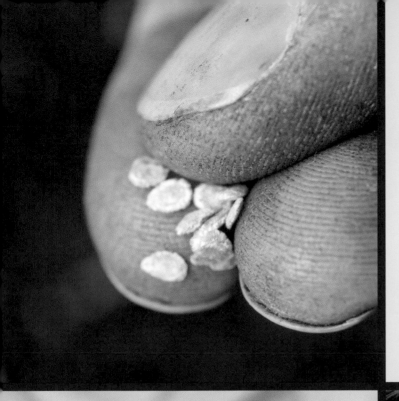

The plants start as seeds. The seeds grow into small plants called seedlings.

Have you ever grown a plant outside in a garden?

LET'S VISIT A TOMATO GARDEN

A gardener plants the seedling in soil.

The roots take in water from the soil. The leaves take in sunshine for energy.

Soon, flowers appear on the plants.

Tiny green fruits grow from the flowers. These are tomatoes!

Do you think these tomatoes are ready to eat?

13

Tomatoes change color as they grow. Many turn red.

Tomatoes can also be yellow, green, and even purple!

These tomatoes are ripe.
This means they are fully
grown and ready to pick.

How many different colors do you see?

A gardener picks the tomatoes.

The gardener washes the tomatoes.

She will use them to make pasta sauce.

What would you do with ripe tomatoes?

LET'S COOK

Always have an adult present when working in the kitchen!

EASY TOMATO SAUCE

INGREDIENTS

- 1 tablespoon olive oil
- 1 small onion, finely chopped
- 1 garlic clove, finely chopped
- 2 pounds (900 g) whole tomatoes, cored
- 2 tablespoons Italian parsley, minced

1. Warm the olive oil in a saucepan over medium heat.

2. Add the chopped onion and garlic. Cook until softened, about 5 minutes.

3. Add the tomatoes and parsley. Cover the saucepan with a lid and turn the heat down to medium-low.

4. Cook the tomatoes for about 20 minutes. They will begin to lose their shape.

5. Allow the tomatoes to cool completely.

6. Puree the mixture using a blender or food processor.

7. Enjoy the sauce on a pizza or with pasta.

SEE THIS RECIPE IN ACTION!

LET'S MAKE

TOMATO SLICE SEEDLING

MATERIALS

- slice of tomato
- potting soil
- container with small holes for drainage
- spray bottle
- water

1. Fill the container a little more than halfway with potting soil.

2. Place the tomato slice on top of the soil. Cover the tomato with a layer of soil.

3. Gently press down the soil in the container.

4. Spray the soil with water until it is moist.

5. Place the container in a sunny spot inside or outside. When the soil looks dry, spray it gently with water.

6. In about 2 weeks, a seedling should sprout. Transfer it to a larger pot.

Let's Read

Colossal Questions—Is a Tomato a Fruit or a Vegetable?
https://www.youtube.com/watch?v=9m81GlfA1BE

Florida Tomatoes—Terra's Adventure Guide
https://www.floridatomatoes.org/kids-corner/

James, Dawn. *Turning Tomatoes into Ketchup*. New York: Cavendish Square Publishing, 2014.

Musgrave, Ruth. *Look & Learn: In My Garden*. Washington, DC: National Geographic Kids, 2017.

National Geographic Kids—10 Top Tomato Facts!
https://www.natgeokids.com/za/discover/science/nature/ten-top-tomato-facts/

Rooney, Anne. *Tomatoes Grow on the Vine*. Mankato, MN: QEB Pub., 2013.

Photo Acknowledgments

The images in this book are used with the permission of: © ARTindividual/iStockphoto, pp. 3 (sauce), 19; © Asia-Pacific Images Studio/iStockphoto, p. 8 (boy); © cpaquin/iStockphoto, p. 23; © Denisfilm/iStockphoto, pp. 3 (ripe tomatoes), 16; © druvo/iStockphoto, p. 14; © EduardSV/iStockphoto, p. 22; © fcafotodigital/iStockphoto, p. 7; © HuyThoai/iStockphoto, p. 15 (purple tomatoes); © JanaShea/iStockphoto, p. 13; © karlisz/iStockphoto, p. 5 (salsa); © katra/iStockphoto, p. 20; © LOVE_LIFE/iStockphoto, p. 7 (various tomato varieties); © martinedoucet/iStockphoto, p. 9 (girl gardening); © Maryviolet/iStockphoto, p. 11; © mfyeung/iStockphoto, p. 7 (girl); © Neyya/iStockphoto, pp. 3 (hand holding seedlings), 9 (hand holding seedlings); © PatrikStedrak/iStockphoto, pp. 3 (flowers), 12; © pinstock/iStockphoto, p. 21; © sam74100/iStockphoto, p. 4; © SwellPhotography/iStockphoto, pp. 3, 9; © TKphotography64/iStockphoto, p. 15; © Tom Merton/iStockphoto, p. 5; © TommL/iStockphoto, p. 17; © tvirbickis/iStockphoto, pp. 1, 6; © undrey/iStockphoto, p. 18; © Vladimir Sukhachev/iStockphoto, p. 15 (yellow cherry tomatoes); © YinYang/iStockphoto, p. 8 (tomato plant isolated); © YuriyS/iStockphoto, p. 10; © zeljkosantrac/iStockphoto, p. 5 (ketchup and fries); © ZoiaKostina/iStockphoto, p. 8.

Cover Photos: © kali9/iStockphoto (girl with tomatoes); © LOVE_LIFE/iStockphoto (tomatoes isolated on white); © tvirbickis/iStockphoto; © zeljkosantrac/iStockphoto (ketchup and fries); © zoranm/iStockphoto (hand picking tomato)